SATAN'S LITTLE INSTRUCTION BOOK

Carmine DeSena

main street books

doubleday

new york   london   toronto

sydney   auckland

SATAN'S little

INSTRUCTION BOOK

A MAIN STREET BOOK
PUBLISHED BY DOUBLEDAY
a division of Bantam Doubleday Dell Publishing Group, Inc.
1540 Broadway, New York, New York 10036

MAIN STREET BOOKS, DOUBLEDAY, and the portrayal of a building with a tree are trademarks of Doubleday, a division of Bantam Doubleday Dell Publishing Group, Inc.

Book design by Dana Leigh Treglia
Illustrations by Mark Matcho

Library of Congress Cataloging-in-Publication Data
DeSena, Carmine.
Satan's little instruction book / Carmine DeSena. — 1st ed.
p.   cm.
"A Main Street book"—T.p. verso.
1. Devil—Humor. I. Title.
PN6162.D418   1996
818'.5402—dc20   95-38485
CIP

ISBN 0-385-48217-5
Copyright © 1996 by Carmine DeSena
All Rights Reserved
Printed in the United States of America
October 1996
1 3 5 7 9 10 8 6 4 2
FIRST EDITION

To my mother, Angelina,
who taught me that *evil*
spelled backward is *live*!

Satan's Little Instruction Book is a collection of all those evil thoughts we have, but are smart enough to keep to ourselves. These thoughts are meant to entertain, and I would never suggest that you actually do them.

—C. D.

EVIL IS AS EVIL DOES!

A special thanks to all those who love and support me despite my evil ways:

Madeline and Joe Agosta; Gil Alicea; Barbara, Jimmy, Jennifer, and Jamie Cestare; Stephanie Cintron and Matt Diamond; Joseph Cintron; Joe, Davida, Jordan, and Logan Cooper; Jennifer and Rose DeSena; Steven Dercole; John Duff; Gregory and Mae Esehak; George Fuller; Sue Fine; Ethel Galowitz; Barbara, Marcelle, and Ina Greenfield; Maryann Irving; Michael Hicks; Jim Jansen; Marie Ibarreta; Frances Jones; Pat Kabram; Tim Kinzler; Tim, Stephanie, and Lauren King; Stephanie Klapper and Steve McCoy; Ian Klapper and Liz Norman; Marilyn, Bruce, and Ari Klickstein; Al and Kathy Krug; Thelma Leibowitz; Thom Lydner; Nedra and Werner Loeb; Ann, Nick, Grace

Ann, Michael, Christine, Nicolas, and Christina LaForgia; Willis Moore; David and Anita Mandel; Nathanial, Carolyn, and Gwendolyn May; Yvonne Negron; Fran Prochak; William Protash; Dan, Heather, and Lemore Raviv; Xivia; Bobby and Maryann Risi; Eddie and Christie; Dee Dee Risi; Nan, Donald, Marilyn, Jimmy, and Kathy Risi; Ron Randolph; Maureen, Steve, Dawn, and Michael Ruiz; Rhina Rogart; Gail Stevens; Connie, Michael, and Dane Seltenrich, Terry Stapelton; Jean, Lou, Carol, Peter, Audra, and Lee Sorman; Carol Schindler; Karen Stahl; Bang Torres; Peg, Neil, Marie, Neil Jr. the fourth, and Connie Twomey; Bruce Tennenbaum; Armand White; Jan Zaccor; Barbara-J Zitwer; and, as always, The Bracci Clan.

Satan's Little Instruction Book

Devilisms to Use on Your Grandparents

- Wear black armbands when you visit.
- Start off every conversation with "Don't you remember we talked about this?"
- Put chili powder in their dental adhesive.
- Explain that a living will has nothing to do with living.
- Frequently ask "Did you see that?"
- Grease their walkers.
- Bring them a vase—then bring up cremation.
- Hide their keys, wallets, and pacemakers.
- Mouth words without speaking.
- Talk about your future and occasionally add "If only you could still be here then."

Devilisms for Use by Dentists

- For a cheery office, decorate the walls—with saws, sledgehammers, and pliers.
- Tell patients you hope they don't mind the loud music. You use it to drown out the screaming.
- Put leg and arm restraints on the exam chair.
- Show slides from your vacation—there's nothing like a captive audience!
- During the cleaning, reapply the plaque.
- Triple the Novocain and force patients to rinse.
- While drilling, create a little topiary.
- Replace the mouth-suction tool with a vacuum.
- As patients revive from the laughing gas, hold up a pair of dentures and say "See, now they are perfect."

Devilisms for use by dental patients

- Announce in the waiting room you heard the dentist doesn't clean his tools.
- When he's giving you Novocain—and warns you that you'll feel a little prick—ask if that costs extra.
- Play Pick-Up-Stix with the dental tools.
- When in the chair, scream as loudly as possible.
- Say "Wow, from this angle you have more hair in your nose than on your head."
- Refuse to take off the gas mask.
- If the dentist asks "Can you feel anything?" say "No, you're just like my husband."
- When he tells you to spit, aim for him.
- Tell him you're on a Tooth Fairy Dental Plan.

Devilisms for a Cruise

- Every time the boat rocks, yell "This is just like *The Poseidon Adventure!*"

- Inflate other people's life jackets during the lifeboat drill.

- After docking, tell other passengers the departure time is an hour later than it is.

- If you see someone getting nauseous, wobble down the hall.

- Talk other guests into playing Frisbee on deck.

- Use the midnight buffet to stage a food fight.

- Befriend the shopaholic passengers to find out what they're sneaking home, then report them to Customs.

Devilisms to use on a politician

- Get even—vote with thought.
- At a rally quiz him to see if he knows his own platform.
- Have campaign buttons made—with his baby picture.
- Vote to make campaign contributions part of income.
- Forget term limits, vote for life limits.
- After a politician has kissed your baby, say he stole the pacifier.
- Tell him that as the economy dips, so should his salary.
- Suggest deducting a percentage of his salary for every campaign promise broken.
- Mandate surprise typing tests for his clerical staff.
- Forget the Contract with America—get a contract with Luigi.

Devilisms for Use by Wives

- During lovemaking, call out his boss's name.
- Talk about your early career in 16mm.
- Use his razor—on the dog.
- In your sleep, mumble "Marvin Mitchelson, Marvin Mitchelson."
- Tell him you wish he were more like k.d. lang.

Devilisms for Use by Husbands

- When she asks for foreplay, get out your golf clubs.
- Don't lift the toilet seat and, most important, don't aim!
- Use *her* razor for a change of pace.
- Forget lipstick on your collar—put a bra in your briefcase.
- Tell her you wish she were more like Harvey Fierstein.

Hellish Holidays—I

- Groundhog Day: Break out the lawn mower.

- Valentine's Day: Give someone a heart but don't tell whose it was.

- Washington's Birthday: Be the father of your country as many times as possible.

- Lincoln's Birthday: Have a theater party.

- February 29: Take a depressed friend to the Empire State Building for Leap Day.

Devilisms to use on hobby types

- Admire a friend's stamp collection—lick the backs.
- Bring fleas to a dog show.
- Tell a sculptor you're into the classics, then rip the arms off his statues.
- Introduce termites into a carpentry shop.
- Ask a model builder for Cindy Crawford.
- Take a bird-watcher to a poultry mart.
- At the next Bake-Off, serve *E. coli* éclairs.
- Draw little numbers on a painter's work.
- Go to Atlantic City—with a friend's coin collection.

Devilisms for Use by an Employer

- Invest the pension plans—at the racetrack.
- Stay open on holidays.
- When office supplies disappear, institute strip searches.
- Put the morning time clock on fast-forward.
- Hold employee-of-the-month contests—and pick yourself as the winner.
- Offer bonuses for employees who rat on each other.
- Have latecomers stand in the corner.
- Consider a picket line an opportunity for hunting without a permit.

Devilisms for use by an employee

- Forget the pens—steal a secretary.
- Sell the company files.
- Slip the names of rising executives to headhunters—and get a piece of the commission.
- Dress for success—make your next suit a discrimination suit.
- Call the EPA about the company's manufacturing plant.
- Unleash asbestos—and get a few days off.
- Collect overtime for commuting.
- Forget coffee breaks—take psychotic breaks.

Devilisms for Use by Parents

- Live long—become a burden.
- Tell your kids you love them as if they were your own.
- Remember: Every criticism you offer is a blow to self-esteem!
- Tell each sibling the other is your favorite.
- Name the kids Tax Deduction One, Tax Deduction Two, and Tax Deduction Three.
- Tell them you only had them because you hate yard work.

Devilisms for Use by Children

- Bring Mom's diaphragm to show-and-tell.
- When your parents ask if you have any questions about sex, ask "How do you do it in a car?"
- Mail parents nursing-home brochures.
- When your parents ask about your future, say "I want to be as famous as John Hinckley."
- Deny them grandchildren.

Beelzebub Bonus!

Remember: Cheating is just luck with brains!

Devilisms for Visiting Italy

- Lean on that Tower of Pisa.
- Grease the Spanish Steps.
- Don't throw three coins in the fountain—fish some change out.
- Put a jockstrap on *David*.
- Try that wet-paper-towel trick in the Sistine Chapel.
- Sneak a velvet Jesus painting into the Vatican art collection.
- Kiss the Pope's ring—and suck out the stone.

Devilish Remarks for a Class Reunion

- "I can't believe you're still alive."
- "You mean you actually married her? Well, I guess we all did—in the biblical sense."
- "Is it twenty years? Your face says forty."
- "Seeing you again makes me see what a waste therapy can be."
- "You look just like your father."
- "I am happy about your life changing—it's the sex change that concerns me."
- "Three kids? Looking at you, I would have thought more."
- "Wow, I had a crush on you and now you could crush me."
- "You give the sixties a bad name."
- "It's great to see you wearing your old football jersey, so . . . I guess nothing much has happened since high school."

New Age Devilisms

- When someone is channeling, tune in the Super Bowl.
- During a group hug, grope someone.
- Forget meditation, stick with sedation.
- When people say they feel your aura, say you can smell theirs.
- Replace someone's wax candles with Roman candles.
- If someone asks to look into your soul, tell the person to look down.
- Send your inner child to bed without supper.
- Tell people about your near-death experience. Then, while they're sleeping, shine a flashlight in their face.
- Forget the tarot thing—read people's credit cards.

Devilisms for use by mechanics

- Rotate the tires back to the same place.
- For a routine inspection, dress like Sherlock Holmes.
- Make customers sit in the car when it's on the lift.
- Show them your dipstick.
- Use vegetable oil for the lube job.
- When you're asked for an estimate, multiply the zeros till their eyes cross.
- Use sanitary napkins for brake pads.
- When you're asked for a new muffler, attach a scarf.
- When car owners describe a strange knocking sound, bring out a band saw and say "Don't worry, I'll find it even if I have to tear this baby apart."

Devilisms to use on your mechanic

- When he's under the hood, pull out the stick.
- Rev the engine when his face is near the radiator.
- Tell him to ignore the screaming from the trunk.
- Reiterate the Golden Rule: Whatever he does to your car you will do to his.
- Ask if he found Junior in the backseat.
- Tell the mechanic to call you at the office with the estimate—then give him the number for the Department of Consumer Affairs.
- Accuse him of changing the radio stations.
- Tell him you lost something in the backseat. When he asks you to describe it, reply with "Well, it was prom night . . ."
- When he's under the car, release the jack.

Devilisms for Use by Teachers

- Distort history.
- Place short students in the back.
- Give surprise quizzes—on material you haven't covered.
- Decorate the room with failing test papers.
- Let it be known that nothing brings a grade up quicker than determination, hard work, and a little cash.
- In science class, use a student to represent "the missing link."
- Hand out summer-school brochures.
- During fire drills, tell certain students to remain seated.
- The day before a test, leave the answer key exposed on your desk—making sure all the answers are wrong.
- Never learn your students' names.

Devilisms for Use by Students

- Glue the erasers together.
- Use your computer class to set up Internet dates.
- At the next assembly meeting, stand next to your favorite teacher and scream "I told you not to touch me like that!"
- On a school trip, sneak a cab home.
- Act confused in sex ed; request an instructional video.
- When asked to erase the board, use an Uzi.
- During drug education class, ask the teacher what they took in the sixties.
- During fire drills, make smores.
- Replace the computer science teacher's curriculum with porn CD-ROMs.
- When told to stay for detention, say "Sure, but it's your turn to bring the condoms."

Beelzebub Bonus!

Remember:
To be really
cruel, be honest
with someone.

Devilisms at a Spa

- Use the steam room to get those pesky wrinkles out of clothes.
- Rub the towels with poison ivy.
- Sell black market candy after meals.
- Drop algae in the hot springs.
- Replace the masseuse's oil with Szechuan oil.
- Add pudding to the mud baths.
- Tell new guests how much weight you've gained since starting the program.

Devilisms to Use on the Bride

- Tell everyone where her father's hiding the shotgun.
- Explain that something borrowed, something blue, shouldn't include the groom.
- Get footprints on her train.
- Tell her how happy she's made the groom—between the wedding gifts and her family's money, he'll be able to pay off some gambling debts.
- Tell her she looks fabulous and is barely showing.
- When she tells you where the honeymoon is to be, respond with "Oh! He took me there too!"
- Decorate the honeymoon car with JUST HAD TO GET MARRIED.
- When she throws the bouquet, bat it back to her.
- After the ceremony, force the bride to be photographed in one of the bridesmaids' dresses.
- Throw fried rice.

Devilisms to Use on the Groom

- Tell him you were as excited to get the invitation as the bride was to get her green card.
- Show his new in-laws a video of his bachelor party.
- Send him the wrong tuxedo.
- Congratulate him on his excellent choice—after all, you taught her everything she knows.
- Hock the rings.
- Flatten the bride's limo tires and tell him she's not coming.
- Tell her family that since that trip to Denmark, the groom's been a new man.
- Toast his virility—acknowledging that at least half the women in the room can concur.
- Snap his cummerbund.

Devilisms for use by lawyers

- Don't wait for an accident case—cause one.
- When held for contempt of court, charge the client by the hour for jail time served.
- For ethical reasons, follow the bar—at least until you fall off the stool.
- When asked the difference between right and wrong, explain that wrong means taking on a client who can't pay.
- Since calls are billable time, keep clients on hold.
- Remember: It's not about right or wrong, it's about intimidation.
- During your summation, throw in some show tunes and a little soft shoe.

Devilisms for use by legal clients

- As your lawyer presents your case, laugh and say "What a great imagination."

- When seated at the defense table, jump up and yell at your lawyer "Watch your hands!"

- About mid-trial, say that you're sleeping with the judge.

- When you've finished testifying, look at your lawyer and say "Did I forget anything?"

- After the lawyer has taken the case on contingency, ask for no damages.

- When the jury is about to convene, recant your testimony.

- As your lawyer gives his summation to the jury, blurt out "Hey, isn't that the dialogue from *Presumed Innocent?*"

Devilisms to use on a sports buff

- As the Super Bowl begins, fake a heart attack.

- During the Olympics, mimic the lighting of the torch ceremony by burning his recliner.

- Plan important events to coincide with every playoff.

- During his busiest time at work, call to say his team is trading a favorite player.

- When he sets the VCR to tape a game or event, switch the channel to PBS.

- Scalp his season tickets.

Devilisms for Visiting Japan

- When invited to a tea ceremony, ask for coffee.

- Let the Japanese know that to present really fresh sushi, they should leave the hooks in.

- Tape MADE IN AMERICA on all their electric appliances.

- Put moths in their kimonos.

- Go to a sumo wrestling match—and initiate a stampede.

- Talk about how much you learned about Japanese culture from watching Godzilla.

- Visit one of Japan's ultramodern factories—to spearhead a union drive.

Devilisms for Thanksgiving

- Tell small children the rich and wonderful Thanksgiving story about how the settlers survived with the help of the Indians whose land they later stole after annihilating thousands.

- Offer to carve the turkey, then use a hockey mask and chain saw.

- Remember cranberry sauce makes a lovely stain.

- Make the most insecure guest sit at the kids' table.

- Ask all your guests to hold hands, close their eyes, and pray for ten minutes—while you go through their coats and purses.

- When guests offer to put bones aside for your dog, explain that the bones *are* your dog.

- After dinner, make an announcement: "Great news, seems my gravy wasn't lumpy after all . . . seems we have a little ant problem in the kitchen."

Beelzebub Bonus!

Party from Hell
Hot Wings Recipe
1 cup barbecue sauce
1 teaspoon hot
   pepper flakes
14 angels

Devilisms for Use by Doctors

- Before giving a physical, submerge your hands in ice water.
- During X rays, whisper "Say cheese."
- On your prescriptions after TAKE ONLY AS DIRECTED, add "I'm a great doctor, but I really want to direct."
- If you're a surgeon, replace the music on your answering machine with the sounds of sawing and screaming.
- Tell patients that in their condition they have to pay in advance.
- When they ask for their next appointment, ask for their next of kin.
- Add black marks to the X rays. Say "Oh, that's probably just a shadow."

Devilisms for Use by Patients

- Slip porno magazines in the waiting room rack.
- Insist on stripping—even for a throat culture.
- If you're kept waiting in the examination room, build a jewelry box from the tongue depressors.
- Bring crayons and draw on the examination room paper.
- Cover the specimen cup loosely.
- When the doctor says "Cough," hack in his face.
- After a rectal exam, ask for a cigarette.
- Explain that if you don't make it, you're taking the doctor with you.
- As you're paying, let the card of a malpractice lawyer fall to the desk.

Devilisms for use by landlords

- Shut off the water during the morning work rush.
- Put up signs for a Hell's Angels meeting in the lobby.
- Install smoke detectors that go off when there's no smoke.
- Create leaks over people's clothes closets.
- Turn the basement into a nightclub.
- On the most frigid day, have the boiler cleaned.
- Store garbage in the elevator.

Devilisms for Use by Tenants

- Before moving out, fill any holes with toothpaste.
- Sublet your place to a grunge band.
- Hold cockfights in the lobby.
- Make snow angels in the plasterboard walls.
- Connect the lights to the plumbing.
- Do the yard work with a machete.
- Get rid of those ugly pipes in the basement.

Supermarket Devilisms

- Open some cookies, chow down, and put the leftovers in someone else's wagon.
- When browsing through the frozen foods, pull the plug.
- Throw embarrassing personal hygiene items in other people's baskets.
- Break one egg in every carton.
- Use your fingernails to ascertain fruit's ripeness.
- Unleash fruit flies in the produce section.
- Change the expiration dates in the dairy section.
- Do your shopping from other people's baskets.
- As the cashier bags, take out the stuff he has already put in.

Devilisms for a Honeymoon

- Tell the bellboy to call you Mrs. Jones—tell the groom you don't know what he's talking about.

- Slip on a sexy nightgown—let her do her own thing.

- Just before lovemaking, switch the DO NOT DISTURB sign with the one that says MAID SERVICE.

- Discuss that open marriage idea.

- Invite everyone from the wedding back to the hotel to check the sheets.

- Tell her it's Dutch treat.

Devilisms at a Movie Theater

- Sit in front of short people.
- When your row is crowded, go to the bathroom frequently.
- Use the usher's flashlight to make shadow puppets on the screen.
- Wear a raincoat during the film—and pant.
- At the film's climax, pinch your baby.
- As you leave, tell the ticket holders' line how the movie ends.

Devilish Postcard Greetings

- Dear Hubby: Surf's up. Sorry about your problem.
- Luv: Paris costs a fortune. Luckily I hocked your jewelry.
- Best Bud: Good news—I'm having a vacation fling. Bad news—it's with your wife.
- Sis: The Mojave can be a barren place—thinking of you.
- Mom: Saw Stonehenge—they used your decorator.
- Wifey: The weather is here. Wish you were beautiful.
- My Dear Son-in-Law: You'd really love Hawaii. Don't worry—I took hundreds of slides.
- Dear Client: The sun is out, the water is blue, and your account is empty.
- Darling: I'm learning how the other half lives—off people like you.

Beelzebub Bonus!

Remember: Stealing is just another word for sharing.

Devilisms at the Beach

- Switch the sunblock with baby oil.
- Relieve yourself when swimming near others.
- When nearby bathers annoy you, throw bread around their blanket to attract seagulls.
- Play Frisbee over children's sand castles.
- Put signs up saying NUDE SUN BATHING ONLY. When the beach is full, call the cops.
- When the sand is piping hot, steal people's sandals.
- As people struggle to change behind towels, yell "I see you!"
- When swimmers ask you to watch their stuff, keep an eye peeled while loading it into your trunk.

Devilisms for Use by a Job Interviewer

- Ask interviewees to get you coffee.

- Tell them not to be anxious, because you have no intention of hiring them.

- Ask them to have a seat—on your lap.

- When reading their résumés, point out any spelling and grammatical mistakes.

- Before a drug screening, ask "What can you cop for me?"

- Exclaim how wonderful the applicants' résumés are—then ask how they feel about lie detector tests.

- Play Truth or Dare.

- Give them ten minutes with a Rubik's Cube.

DEVILISMS FOR USE BY A JOB INTERVIEWEE

- When asked where you hope to be in five years, say "On parole."
- Explain how important an office with a view is.
- When asked about your computer skills, brag about your video game scores.
- Convince the interviewer how much you want the job by saying "I just can't wait to look busy again."
- When asked about your previous job, yell "Nothing was ever proven!"
- When asked if you could be bonded, show your S and M photos.
- Ask if you can review fabric swatches for your office.
- Tell the interviewer you look forward to working at this company because there are so many attractive people to sleep with.

Devilisms for the Subway

- Buy tokens with pennies during rush hour.
- Ask the conductor to make smoke come out of the engine.
- Hold a chin-up contest.
- During those unintelligible announcements, tell passengers you heard we're at war.
- When the subway's really crowded, grope someone.
- When accosted by panhandlers, tell them your problems.
- Whenever the train is going through tunnels, yodel.

Devilisms That Will Change Your Life

- Break old patterns—stalk someone new.
- Befriend co-dependent people and use them.
- Go to a career counselor—ask why he/she can't get a better job.
- Join group therapy, then laugh at the other members' problems.
- Get a pet and teach it to kill.
- Maintain relationships longer—date people with low self-esteem.

Devilisms for Visiting Greece

- Ask if Christina Onassis is what they mean by classic Greek tragedy.
- Serve hemlock on ice, that's nice!
- Open up the Medea Day Care Center.
- When serving the local favorite, lamb, fry up that damn puppet.
- Tack up urban renewal signs at the Parthenon.
- Order a Greek salad—and ask for extra Greeks on it.
- Perk up that grapeleaf recipe with poison ivy.

Devilisms for Prom Night

- At the prom planning meeting, suggest a perky Marquis de Sade theme.

- When buying that prom dress, explain to Mom how something with Velcro is easier to get off in a car.

- Replace the DJ with an oompah band.

- Bring your date a corsage you can smoke.

- If you're using your parents' car, why not take their credit card as well?

- Tell your date you're getting a limo—and hire a hearse.

- Tell her parents not to worry—the hotel rents hourly, so you'll be home early.

- Pull that *Carrie* number.

Devilisms to Use on Your Psychiatrist

- Don't just criticize your mother—bring her in.
- When asked about your father, explain that "I never knew him. He broke his leg and we had to shoot him."
- During the intake interview, pull that scene from *Basic Instinct*.
- Describe sexual fantasies in which the shrink is always a eunuch.
- During regression therapy, make potty on the couch.
- Ask to see her Freudian slip.
- Bring a bong to group therapy.
- Ask about malpractice insurance.
- Become self-actualized—don't pay for your session.

Devilisms for Psychiatrists to Use on Their Patients

- Begin the session with "Hurry up, there are *some* people I want to talk to."
- Leave rejection-obsessed patients alone in the office.
- Explain that you met their mother and she's lovely, so the problem must be theirs.
- After patients describe their most intimate fantasies, respond with "That's disgusting!"
- Give out only those psychiatric medications that cause weight gain.
- During group therapy, ask the participants if they're sick of one another.
- Tell patients to speak softly because you'll be napping.
- Finish the session with "Tell it to someone who cares."

Beelzebub Bonus!

Devilish affirmation: I will lie to, steal from, and manipulate a new person every day.

Department Store Devilisms

- Go to the information desk and ask "Where do babies come from?"
- Why buy light bulbs? Just visit the lamp department.
- Go to the small-appliance department and ask if they carry marital aids.
- Fake a seizure in the crystal department.
- Bring your bed-wetting junior to the mattress sale.
- At the bridal registry, register the groom with lots of different women.
- Laugh at people getting makeovers.
- Take that new puppy, Spot, for a walk in the oriental rug department.
- As people are leaving, throw merchandise sensors in their shopping bags.

More devilisms for use by parents

- While the children are at school—move!
- Compare them to friends' "successful" children.
- Don't tell them where babies come from.
- Leave everything to charity.
- Explain that children should be seen and not heard, so they should really try to be more attractive.
- Say "You were such a cute baby—too bad about that puberty thing."

More devilisms for use by children

- Make parents notice you—steal their car.
- Find their hidden porno stash and show company.
- If they wait up for you, park the car where they can see it—in the living room.
- Get accepted to expensive, prestigious Ivy League schools, then say you have to "find yourself."
- At family gatherings, ask "Uncle Johnny, what's a deadbeat? Dad said you would know."
- Tell parents "Nature or nurture—either way, it's your fault."

Devilisms for a Baby Shower

- Give the future mommy a birthing video—a cut from *Rosemary's Baby*.

- Talk about how nice her old hips were.

- Give her baby sweaters with three arms—say you saw the amnio.

- When she explains how her husband has agreed to do half the feedings, laugh hysterically.

- Give a mobile that plays "Tomorrow."

- Play a party game—Name the Baby's Father.

Devilisms to Use on Your Blind Dates

- Begin the evening by handing them a "What to do if I have a seizure" note.

- Let them know you can't deny them the special gift that is you.

- Offer to take them to dinner—use your fast-food coupons.

- Ask if they believe in love at first sight. If they say yes, show them your genitals.

- Bring your mother—explain she's going to pay.

- Make it a real blind date—go for their eyes.

- Explain that you normally never have sex on the first date, but since you have only a week to live . . .

- Tell them you give great personality.

Devilisms at a Factory

- Fix the break bell to ring every ten minutes.
- Put lice in the hair nets.
- Wear a surgical mask and walk around with a toxic-fumes report.
- After a day in Food Production, tell the foreman you lost your Band-Aid.
- During coffee breaks, glue the disassembled parts to the conveyer belt.
- Tell your co-workers the new guy is really an efficiency expert.
- At a bottling factory, stuff messages into bottles.

Devilisms for use by Beauticians and Hair Stylists

- Dye their back hair a different color.

- If people engage you in boring chitchat, laughingly refer to the time you slaughtered your family with a pair of scissors.

- When clients ask for a new look, say two words: "Hair weave."

- Switch the hair gel and the depilatory cream.

- Forget the hair dryer—use a blow torch.

- Tell people their new hairstyle is meant to be seen in dim light.

Hellish Holidays—II

- April 15: Cheat on your taxes—the government cheats on you.

- Mother's Day: Call your mother and tell her what a good time you had with your dad and new stepmom.

- Father's Day: Send him a card beginning "Dear Sperm Donor."

- Easter: Serve rabbit stew.

- Arbor Day: Save a tree, kill a logger.

Devilisms for Visiting China

- Go to the Great Wall and spray-paint your name.
- Ask what exactly is taboo in the Forbidden City.
- Tell fellow travelers you notice a general scarcity of cats.
- Ask if people who live on boats eat "junk food."
- Knock on people's doors and ask for takeout.
- Ask if the Cultural Revolution meant they finally got television.
- When in Peking, yell "Duck!"

Devilisms for an Airplane

- Change the destination tickets on other people's suitcases.

- In a loud voice, ask the stewardess if you can barbecue in that wing fire.

- Tell your fellow passengers "Wow, I just met the pilot in the bar and, boy, can he hold his liquor!"

- Steal people's peanuts.

- Cut the bottoms off the air-sickness bags—and hope for turbulence.

- As the movie begins, tell everyone the ending.

- If the person in the seat next to you is hogging the armrest, apply glue to it while he/she is in the bathroom.

Devilisms just between friends

- Meet ugly people in bars and give them your friend's business card.

- Send a friend to the bank after putting a robbery note in with the deposit slip.

- Tell a friend his/her lover made a play for you, but made you promise not to mention it.

- Offer a personal loan, then sell the agreement to a loan shark.

- After you gain friends' trust, use their confidences to juice up party gossip.

- Lend them your car for their road test—grease the brakes.

- When you see the new baby, exclaim "She looks just like your mother-in-law!"

- Spend hours making 1-900 calls from friends' phones.

Beelzebub Bonus!

Remember:
Idle hands are the
devil's plaything—
when in public,
touch yourself.

Devilisms at a Dry-Out Clinic

- Spike the water fountain.

- Engage your encounter group in a rousing chorus of "One Hundred Bottles of Beer on the Wall."

- Be sensitive to the fact that these patients are incredibly vulnerable. It's a great time to start a floating crap table and addict them to gambling.

- Offer a celebrity film festival featuring Judy Garland, John Belushi, and Elvis.

- If a patient is recovering nicely, plant drugs in his/her room.

- In group therapy, if they say they feel unloved, counter with "Who could love a junkie?"

Devilisms for Use by a Receptionist

- Play the I Can't Hear You game. Yell, "Hello, hello. Is anybody there?"

- Put everyone on hold forever—take his/her name again each time you pick up the line.

- Play Switch a Digit on phone messages.

- Remember: If you can access people's voice mail, you can blackmail your way up the corporate ladder.

- Pretend to be a phone-sex business—and get some credit card numbers.

- When spouses call and ask where they can reach their loved ones, give them the names of motels that rent by the hour.

- Forget "Can you hold, please." Instead, say "This number has been disconnected."

How to be a houseguest from hell

- Upon arrival, list your food allergies.
- Say "My room is beautiful—where's the disinfectant?"
- Even though you're off but they're working, hog the bathroom every morning.
- Treat the place like a hotel—steal the towels.
- When they're at work, start a worldwide long-distance calling service from their phone.
- Treat your hosts to your organizational skills—rearrange the furniture, their finances, and their children's lives.
- Order all the cable channels.
- Borrow their car—and forget where you left it.
- You'll need souvenirs. Besides the towels, see what cute and costly things they've collected.
- Seduce the spouse of your choice.

Devilisms to use on a bald man

- For Christmas, give him a membership to the fruit-of-the-month club—twelve months of melons.

- Say "Wait! Hold still!" Reapply lipstick using his head as a mirror.

- Ask if he knows Beldar.

- Play connect the dots with his head moles.

- Buy him car wax.

- Paint a bull's-eye on his head while he sleeps—then get suction darts.

Devilisms at the Circus

- Put cotton candy in people's hair.
- Compare the bearded lady to your mother-in-law.
- Buy other people's children those dangerous circus whips.
- Point the human cannon toward the wall.
- Bring your children to the freak show—offer to sell them.
- Point out the sword swallower to your wife.

More devilisms for use by an employer

- Greet employees every morning with "Hello, deadwood."
- Move their desks into the parking lot.
- Have an office party—and don't invite them.
- Explain that the company's not going for layoffs, they are.
- When unhappy with their work, slap their hands with a ruler.
- Tell them they have been reassigned—then give them mops and brooms.
- Arrange a "Best of luck, sorry to see you go" party for them weekly.
- Put "Do not open—party deceased" on their paychecks.

More devilisms for use by an employee

- Put a picture of the boss's wife on your desk.
- Wear a swimsuit to the secretarial pool.
- When criticized by your supervisor, say "I know you are, but what am I?"
- Forget the Walkman, bring a boom box.
- The next time you have a cold, sneeze on the boss's tie.
- When the boss asks to see you, tell him to make an appointment.
- On the office phones, "reach out and touch someone"—in Asia.

Devilisms at a Restaurant

- Walk through the restaurant picking food off other people's plates.
- Ask to join people you don't know—then stick them with your check.
- When the busboy's tray is filled, play Dish Toss.
- Ask to change tables every fifteen minutes.
- When dining at a Mexican place, remove all the toilet paper from the bathroom.
- Loosen the tops on the salt and pepper.
- Try the old pull-the-table-cloth-off-a-set-table trick.
- Have the waitperson wrap up even the tiniest of leftovers, but leave it on the table.
- Leave the tip under an upside-down glass of water.

Beelzebub Bonus!

Remember: Angels have wings so they can get *out* of heaven.

More devilisms for use by wives

- Keep a list of the hottest delivery boys.
- Start an education fund for Lorena Bobbitt.
- Fax him at work about finally getting him that appointment at a fertility clinic.
- Pair all of his socks one black, one blue, one black . . .
- Ask him to call your old boyfriend because "he really knew how to do it."
- Barter sex for household chores.

More devilisms for use by husbands

- Tell her that in the beauty pageant of life she's Miss Congeniality.
- Get that O.J. T-shirt.
- Always ignore directions, especially during sex.
- Put holes in her new packages of stockings.
- Tell her how much you think foot binding would help your relationship.
- After your orgasm, suggest she finish up on her own.

Devilisms for Visiting France

- Loosen some screws on the Eiffel Tower.
- Ask for ketchup.
- Tell tour guides you find Monet derivative.
- Go right on the Left Bank.
- When something costs eight francs, give them a pack of Hebrew Nationals.
- Charge your hotel to Charles de Gaulle.
- Visit Chanel—ask for hot cocoa.

Devilisms at the Ballet

- Ask if Twyla Tharp is the girl that Al Sharpton was defending.
- See *Swan Lake*—bring a shotgun.
- Ask the conductor to pick up the pace.
- When the dancers are on point, yell "Hey, they're using wires!"
- Ask when the dancers are going to do that kick line thing.
- Yell for the dancers to speak up.

Devilisms for use by the plumber

- Ask customers if they want to see your plumber's snake.
- Hook up the washing machine and the toilet to the same line.
- Tell panicked customers they should really start a salmon farm.
- Pitch a new combination cess/swimming pool.
- Go to anxious customers wearing a wet suit.
- Put a baby alligator in the toilet.
- Connect the pipes in a useless—but artistic—fashion.
- Leave everything running.
- Attach a surprise bidet feature to the toilet flusher.
- Ask customers if they have life preservers.

Devilisms for a Camping Trip

- Pour honey on a friend's tent.
- Throw firecrackers into the campfire.
- Send people hiking—and give them the wrong map.
- Go fishing in the reserve hatchery.
- When it's open season, shoot a hunter.
- Bring a shovel so you can add to your home garden.
- Point out a great swimming hole—make sure it's next to rapids.
- Build a lean-to, making sure it's collapsible.
- Ask the park rangers where you can sight some deer, then invite them for venison.

Hellish Holidays—III

- Memorial Day: Send someone a tombstone.

- Labor Day: Bust a union.

- St. Patrick's Day: Serve moldy food, saying the green comes from food coloring.

- Christmas Day: Buy them presents they can't return.

- December 31: Pick your resolutions from this book.

Beelzebub Bonus!

Remember: Being vindictive is just asserting yourself.

Devilisms for Breaking Up with Lovers

- When things start going badly, start renting serial-killer movies.
- Give them half of everything they co-paid for—use a rotary saw.
- Demand half the pet.
- Confess that there were always problems—that's why you slept around so much.
- When friends ask "What happened?" reply "When he said he was into animal husbandry, I thought he wanted to be a vet."
- Get a tax break, donate their things to charity.
- Remember those nude photos you took? I think we have this year's Christmas card picture!

Devilisms at an All-Night Convenience Store

- Apply FAT FREE stickers to the frozen burritos.
- Put real slush in the snow cones.
- Switch the mustard and ketchup signs at the condiment bar.
- Tell the cashier you're from Immigration.
- At the self-service counter, switch the regular and decaf coffees.
- Unwrap the porno magazines.
- When traveling, use the microwave to dry your hand-washed undies.
- Do the "Dance of the Seven Veils" in front of the security camera.

Devilisms to Use on the Baby-Sitter

- Sneak in extra kids—charge their parents.

- Wait outside till the sitter's boyfriend arrives—tell him he'll have to take a number.

- Put price tags on the food, as in a hotel fridge.

- Let the fact that you have a pet rottweiler slip your mind.

- Call several times to say "Have you checked the children?"

- Tell her not to worry, the priest exorcised little Johnny this morning.

- Alarm the liquor cabinet.

- At midnight, call and say "I can't take it anymore—I'm going to Paris!"

Devilisms for use by the Baby-Sitter

- Rent the parents' second car out for the evening.

- Find their credit card bills—and shop by mail.

- Have the kids set up a yard sale and sell some appliances.

- Use the fridge to food-shop for your boyfriend.

- Let the kids stay up—to give you a manicure.

- Invite your friends to a cash bar.

- Put up a HOUSE FOR SALE sign in the yard.

- Call parents in the middle of dinner—to ask about their home owner's policy.

Devilisms for a Jewelry Store

- Test the diamonds by monogramming the showcase.

- If they offer free ear piercing, ask if they do genital piercing.

- Ask them to size you for toe rings.

- Change the time on the clock in the watch-repair section.

- Tell them you're the oysters' defense lawyer—they want their pearls back.

- Go for appraisals—with a squirt ring.

- Ask if you can buy semiprecious stones with your semiprecious coin collection.

- Show the family jewels.

Devilisms for Use by Hospital Staff Members

- Visit upcoming surgery patients with blood-soaked gowns.
- Hook up people's heart monitors to video games.
- Play switchies with the patient charts in the ICU.
- Cover sleeping patients' faces with sheets, then act shocked when they awaken.
- Give sponge baths at 110 degrees.
- Tell new parents that for ten dollars extra they can have the pick of the litter.
- When doing a leg cast, think surrealism.
- Wheel all the hospital beds into the hall for a rousing game of bumper cars.

Devilisms for Visiting England

- Make London Bridge fall down.
- Send Prince Charles a copy of *Dumbo*.
- Go to Piccadilly Circus—and ask to see the clowns.
- Bring a barbecue starter to Madame Tussaud's wax museum.
- At Buckingham Palace, ask to see the Royal Family Jewels.
- Drive on the right.
- Ask the guard at Windsor Palace for directions.

Beelzebub Bonus!

Remember: Adultery means you're of age.

Devilisms for Jury Duty

- Ask if you can bang the gavel.
- Sing the following in the jury box: "Twelve people in a box and the alternate came in and said, 'Move over, move over,' so they all moved over and the first juror fell out. 'Move over, move over . . .' "
- Ask the judge what he's wearing under his robe.
- In the middle of the defendant's testimony, yell "Sure, and I'm the Queen of England!"
- During breaks, pull out a copy of *Twelve Angry Men*.
- In the middle of crucial testimony, look around the jury box and say "Okay, who cut the cheese?"
- When an attorney objects, yell "Well, it's about time!"
- Ask if you can weigh yourself on the scales of justice.
- After the lawyers finish their summations, hold up rating numbers.

You know your blind date was arranged in hell when:

- They say they'll be carrying a copy of *Siddhartha*.
- They want to meet in an alley.
- They tell you their nickname is the "Latex Lover."
- They say they like Lap Dancing—and they mean from Finland.
- They quote The Fonz.
- They tell you not to call late because Mom is a light sleeper.
- Their greatest sexual fantasy is playing dentist.
- They set the hour for the date to end as "pumpkin time."
- *They have a tail.*

Devilisms at a Video Store

- Ask the clerks to suggest their favorite films, then laugh at their taste.
- Replace the classic films with home movies.
- Forget rewind—try unwind.
- Hide new releases in the educational film section.
- Swipe tapes from the return bin.
- At the register, point out people renting adult films.
- Remember that video boxes make great bathtub floats.

Devilish Baby Compliments

- "Yes, he's very special. In fact, I think he'll probably go to a very special school."
- "She looks just like her father—has he seen her yet?"
- "He's so animated, or is that a seizure?"
- "Look how he follows me with his eyes, just like a little stalker."
- "She's your first—nice try."
- "Oh, I'm sure he's very intelligent—there's always one good feature."
- "I'm sure his head will grow into those ears."
- "As she gets older, she'll sleep through the night—always with different people, but definitely through the night."
- "That bonnet is adorable, but it could use a veil."

Devilisms to use on a feminist

- Tell her what a babe she is.
- If she disputes "a woman's place is in the home," evict her.
- Agree with a woman's right to choose and a man's right to ignore.
- Replace her herbal tea with caffeinated.
- Tell her you thought the women's movement was a symphony.
- When she goes clothes shopping, report her to NOW.
- When she says a woman can do anything as well as a man, have her belch.
- Tell her you *expect* her to make more money than you.
- Steal her cat.

Devilisms to Use on a Male Chauvinist Pig

- Comment on his feminine side.
- When he brings up that breadwinner shtick, tell him to make you a sandwich.
- Review that cars-overcompensating-for-penis-size theory.
- Have him open his beer with his teeth.
- When he says women are the weaker sex, show him your C-section scars.
- Replace his sports channel with the Home Shopping Network.
- Agree that nothing *is* better than a man.
- When he argues men can do anything better than women, say "Okay, have a baby."
- Ask him to fix something—the cat.

Beelzebub Bonus!
Holiday Presents from Hell

- Irregular pets.
- Large bottles of it-smells-almost-like-the-real-thing cologne.
- A Chia Pet toilet seat.
- Eight-track tapes.
- Don't forget last year's uneaten cheese-log-and-smoked-sausage baskets!
- Oh, those Barry Manilow records!

Devilisms for the Highway

- Replace your headlights with strobes.
- Put a tape recorder of people screaming in the trunk.
- Tailgate—even when there's no traffic.
- When a car is next to you, pick your nose.
- Pull a Chinese fire drill.
- Have your rider hold up a note saying I'M BEING KIDNAPPED BY ALIENS.
- At rest stops, switch the IN and OUT signs.
- Ask workers at tollbooths if they have any Toll-House cookies.

Devilish Toasts

- "We just can't stop talking about you."

- "May your marriage last as long as the ceremony."

- "To your health, wherever it's gone."

- "Remember graduation isn't just the end of school. It's the beginning of unemployment."

- "Thirty isn't the end of everything, just most things."

- "On your wedding day, remember love conquers all—but you'll need a lawyer for a settlement."

- "What can I say about a person who has everything—except time."

Devilisms to do while others are toasting

- Yell "You say that about everyone!"
- Hold up a tissue and point to their nose.
- Start applauding before they finish.
- Signal them that there is something on their teeth.
- When they finish, raise your glass and ask "Does that mean you're still sleeping with them?"
- At the crucial moment, get friends to yawn.
- When they finish, yell "Encore!"

Devilisms for Use by Cops

- Pull motorists over—because you can.
- Use a hand buzzer when frisking.
- Forget the stun gun—use a curling iron.
- Ask them to spread-eagle, then pinch an inch.
- During the mug shots, tell suspects to wet their lips.
- Fingerprint them with indelible ink.
- Tell them how much you like the handcuff part.
- Put a skeleton in the holding cell.

Devilisms to Use on Cops

- When they flash their badges, flash them.
- After they read you your rights, ask if you can stay up for another story.
- On the way to police headquarters, ask if you can ring the siren.
- In the backseat of the car, bang your head against the window, then claim police brutality.
- During the mug shots, ask for some wallet size for your family.
- When you're being fingerprinted, touch them.
- Tell them how much you like the handcuff part.
- During a search when they say "Spread them," answer "Not without dinner."

Devilisms to use on trophy wives

- Round up party guests and play Find the Real Root Color.
- Admire their combination engagement/teething ring.
- Ask if their husbands have to sign their report cards.
- Tell them you want to see what their husbands see in them— ask them to lie down.
- Ask if CPR was part of the wedding vows.
- Suggest "The Other Woman" for their wedding song.

Devilisms for the Emergency Room

- As the waiting area fills, put out a tip cup with a sign that says SUGGESTIONS FOR FASTER SERVICE.
- Tell patients that all their agonizing screams are giving you a headache.
- Forget stitches—do embroidery.
- Tell the patients their Medicaid cards are maxed out.
- As you examine people, consult *How to Be a Doctor in Just Three Weeks*.
- Release wheelchair brakes.
- Greet family members with "I'm sorry there was nothing I could do."
- Set up the Muzak to pulse with the ambulance lights. Yell "Everybody hustle!"
- When the waiting room is crammed with patients, yell "Is there a doctor in the house?"

Beelzebub Bonus!
Devil Activities

- **At a funeral, draw a happy face on the corpse.**
- **Be sure to mail your friends copies of all the photos where their eyes are red and their chins have doubled.**
- **Send flowers to people with hay fever.**
- **Refill "designer" water bottles from the toilet.**
- **Send your friends magazine subscriptions. Check BILL ME LATER.**

Devilisms for a Funeral

- Bring hankies for the mourners—sprayed with Mace.
- Put baby bumpers around the casket.
- Point out the deceased's mistress.
- Grease the coffin handles.
- At an open casket ceremony, jump and yell "Hey, he moved!"
- During a flowery eulogy, snort and say "Yeah, right."
- Take the funeral car brigade through a fast-food drive-through window.
- At the wake, tell the families there's a gravediggers' strike and they'll have to pitch in.
- When you greet the widow, ask "What's for lunch?"

Devilisms to use on authors

- Ask for a signed copy of their book, then slip a check under the pen.

- Tell them your favorite part of their book is the cover.

- Ask who the original author was.

- Say you can hardly wait to pick up a copy at the remainder table.

- Explain that theirs are stories that should be told only when everyone else is drunk.

- Tell them their work makes you want to save trees.

- Explain that their book is a natural for libraries—they have to buy everything.

Devilisms to use on editors

- Don't use your spell-check.
- Forget the punctuation—claim that it's stream of consciousness.
- When meeting to hear about revisions, wear army gear.
- When they comment that a character seems cold and unsympathetic, say "But it was based on you!"
- When they tell you what they don't like about your writing, say you feel the same about the way they talk.
- Whenever they say "That could never happen," show them videos of your life.
- Dedicate your book to them and "other destroyers of art and culture."

Beelzebub Bonus!

Remember: Guilt is a useless emotion unless you can inflict it on others.

FIN

ABOUT THE AUTHOR

Carmine DeSena describes himself as a "New Yawker." His love for the city's diversity is reflected in his writing. His books include humor, *Lies: The Whole Truth*; autobiography, *The Air Down Here: True Tales of a South Bronx Boyhood* (coauthor); and "how to," *The Comedy Market: A Writer's Guide to Making Money Being Funny*. As a journalist, he has written on science, health, and the arts for periodicals that include the *New York Times*, *Us* magazine, and *Theater Week*. In addition, he has been active on the New York comedy scene as a performer with the improvisation group OK, So We Lied, and his sketch material has been aired nationally on the ABC radio network. Carmine reports that he remains "grounded" despite his creative endeavors by his work as a Certified Rehabilitation Counselor. In this capacity, he supervises a program helping psychiatrically disabled adults return to the community.

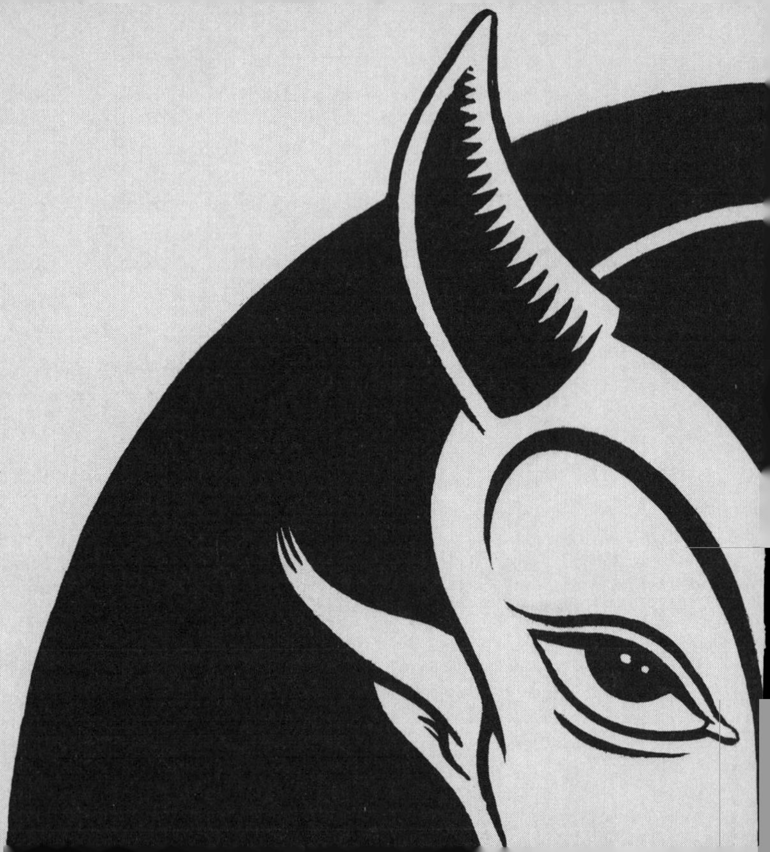

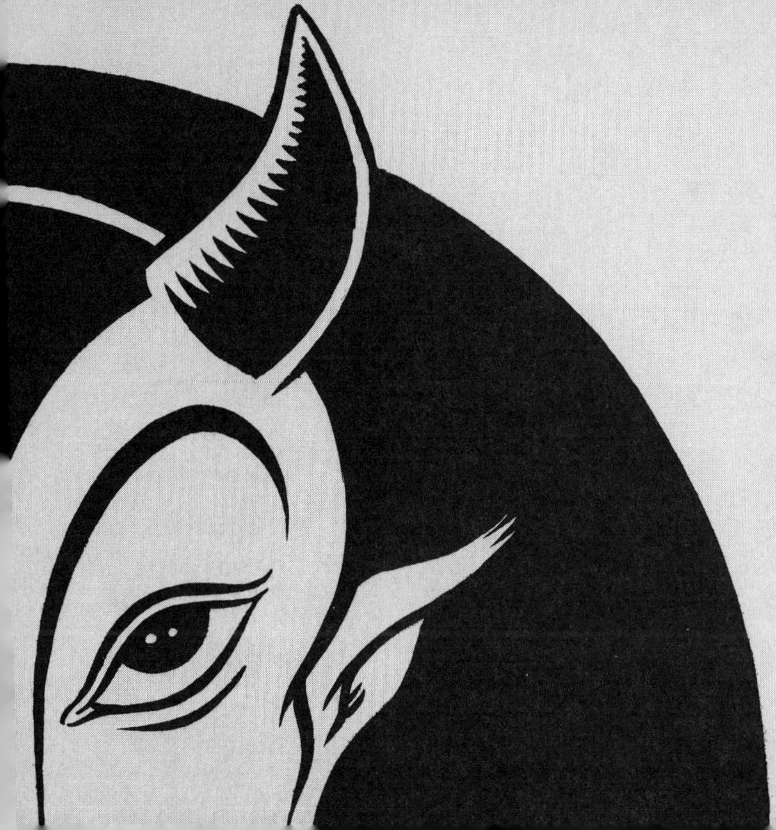